Dear Graduate

Written by Judy Smith

Photography by Lou Guarracino

Education Starts Now

To be successful, you must be a lifelong learner. Never stop increasing your education whether it is in school, reading or studying. There is always something new to learn.

Persevere

Believe everything happens for a reason. Sounds trite, but it's true. Refuse to allow anyone or anything to strip you of the ability to always see and believe in hope. Every experience in life - positive or negative - is an opportunity to grow and change.

Embrace Failure

You will fail at some point, at something. Don't hope or plan for it, but do expect it. If you're making mistakes, it means you're doing something. The only people who don't make mistakes are those who don't try anything.

Follow Your Own Path

There will be others with you on your path through life, guiding and comforting you. However, the lessons you learn on your travels are truly yours alone. The most important relationship you will ever have with anyone is with yourself.

Generosity

Give more to others than they expect, and do so willingly.

Friendship

Surround yourself with others who value and appreciate you. All you need are a few "real" people in your life who truly understand and love you.

Getting off the Couch

Move, dance, play, run, and soar.

Gratitude

Be thankful for what you have — health, family, shelter, food.

Be thankful for what you don't have — illness, loneliness, homelessness.

Appreciate Yourself

Your happiness and self-worth are not dependent on what others may think of you. Make the conscious decision that you have faith in yourself and your abilities. The moment you begin to believe in yourself, things will change rapidly.

Art of Acceptance

Accepting a difficult situation as it is doesn't mean you agree
with it, only that you understand you are not able to change it.
You can only change how you allow it to affect you.

Be in the Moment

Focus on one task at a time rather than trying
to accomplish everything at once.

Change Your Attitude

Alter the way you view things and the things you
are having issues with will be altered. Changing
your attitude is always the quickest route to
changing your life.

Enjoy the Journey

Goals are important but not at the expense of your happiness.
Maintain a balance between getting to where you want to go
and being happy as you get there.

Don't Keep up with the Joneses

Things won't make you happy. Memories will. Avoid going into debt just to have a new car or the latest and greatest gadgets.

Have Order in Your Life

Order welcomes calmness in your life which precedes clear thought. This allows room in our lives for happiness and success. When your mind is clear, you can make room for greater happiness and success. Clarity comes when there is order in the space where you exist.

Have you read any good books lately?

Not only is reading a mind expanding exercise, it also removes us from our daily lives. Search for new hobbies, expand your vision and let your mind soar. Read often – *it's magical!*

Must Reads:

- *Don Quixote* by Miguel de Cervantes
- *Moby Dick* by Herman Melville
- *Great Gatsby* by F. Scott Fitzgerald
- *The Prince* by Niccolo Machiavelli
- *Catcher in the Rye* by J.D. Salinger
- *How to Cook Everything* by Mark Bittman
- *Catch 22* by Joseph Heller
- *Lord of the Rings* by J.R.R. Tolkien
- *Walden* by Henry David Thoreau
- *Secrets of Closing the Sale* by Zig Ziglar
- *How to Win Friends and Influence People* by Dale Carnegie
- *1984* by George Orwell
- *A Brief History of Time* by Stephen Hawking
- *The Sun Also Rises* by Ernest Hemingway
- *Siddhartha* by Hermann Hesse
- *To Kill a Mockingbird* by Harper Lee

Learning from Criticism

Do not ignore criticism, it helps you grow and develop. Respond in a calm and positive manner and remove emotions from the equation. Do not allow your sense of ego to stand in the way of objectively reviewing the comments. This will open the door to accept constructive criticism and ultimately improve the quality of your life.

Live Simply

Practice the art of living simply by having things in your home and your office arranged in a way that will relax and energize you.

Live the Lifestyle

Having money is not the key to happiness, however it does provide the self-sufficiency needed to give you the freedom to share yourself creatively and freely without worry.

Always remember:

What you save is more important than what you earn.

Share your good fortune with others when they need it.

Respect the things you have and avoid waste.

Mentally live the lifestyle you desire.

Networking

Stay in touch with people you respect. Welcome opportunities, personally and professionally. Constantly seek to get to know people from different backgrounds and life experiences.

Fortify Your Soul

Make wise choices in your diet.

Exercise often.

Sleep on the same schedule as much as possible.

Be Passionate

Everyone has their own unique talents, passions and gifts. The earlier you discover and develop yours, the easier success will come to you. If you are passionate about what you do, it will never seem like "work."

Dare to Dream

Unless you dream, it won't come true. Expand your visions
and let your mind explore.

Pursue the Right Career

Be passionate about your job and choose a career that will fulfill you and bring happiness. When we follow our authentic path, we are using gifts that have been bestowed upon us. By seeking wonder and exploring your passions, the money will follow. Your career should inspire, satisfy and reward you.

Financial Know How

Learn about financial topics to gain functional knowledge of personal finance. Learn how the tax system works.

Save Now?
Yes, start saving for your retirement right now! Saving as little as two percent of your income into a money market account will yield an amazing amount when it comes time for your retirement. If your employer offers any type of matching program, take advantage of it.

Unplug

Do not allow
technology
to rob you of
the experience
of real living.

There is an entire
universe looming
out there woven
together by
sun, clouds,
mountains and
valleys. Explore it,
experience it.

Rejoice in Your Individuality

No one else is exactly like you.

Sometimes You Win, Sometimes You Lose

Win without acting like it's the first time you have won.

Lose without losing control.

Sounds of Silence

Laying deep in your soul, tucked away from all of life's interruptions, is golden silence leading to your dreams. There lie your passions, your secrets, your bliss. Try and find that place every day with just a few moments of silence. Listen to what the stillness is saying to you.

Towing
the Line

Give more than
what is expected.
Work an extra
half hour or more
than required.

Truth be Told

Always be true to
yourself and you will
never feel the need
to be false to others.

Try Something New...Often

Growth comes when we step out of our comfort zone.

Believe in Yourself

Believe in yourself first and others will believe in you as well. Believe in all that you are and all that you strive to be.

What Would You Do if You Knew You Could Not Fail?

Imagine not having the fear to do the things you want to do in life. Today, at this very moment, you have the ability, wisdom and strength to be all you want to be and have all your dreams come true. Trust in yourself, toss fears aside and let the hues of your bright future shine through.

- *Your greatest success will come as a result of a previous failure.*
- *Participate in life- never withdraw.*
- *Never give up…this is not an option.*

Walking
in Peace

Walking will cure
most problems,
refresh your soul
and provide
moments of
serenity to clear
your mind.

Welcome a New Day!

Enjoy the early morning hours with peace, quiet and reflection by taking a few minutes to simply breathe. The most glorious part of the day is the sunrise when the day slowly gets brighter, when the dark blue sky turns a lighter hue and the brilliant colors seep into the sky. Breathe in the glory of a new day.

Venus and Mars

Love is as natural and vital to life as breathing. It is as crucial for your mind and body as the air you breathe. The more connected you are to the people in your life, the healthier you will be physically and mentally.

Fall in love when you are ready, not when you are lonely.

Love is not perfect. It is full of good times, hard times and times when you simply want to give up.

Sincere love is finding someone who will protect, respect and appreciate you.

When you love, love openly and unconditionally.

Love conquers all…however, you must surrender to it first.

True love is unconditional where we accept each other's flaws and embrace each other's differences.

Love is complete peace and excruciating, almost unbearable joy and the deep passionate sense of being "home".

Be Frugal

Live frugally for as long as you can before marriage, home owner-
ship and children enter your life. Build your credit history slowly
by opening accounts and paying them off promptly.

Go Forth and Explore!

Don't be confined to the borders of your town, state or country. Travel is often best during your formidable years prior to the demands of family life, so go forth! Keep an open mind and an open heart and embrace the cultures and differences you find. Grasp every opportunity to travel overseas.

Mountain Climbing

Now is the time to explore your wildest passions and dreams. You have more free time now than you ever will and your body is more apt to cooperate now than when you are older.

Find A Mentor

Observe the most successful people around you, and seek wisdom
and advice from those who have walked the path before you.
After all, they have already "been there, done that!"

Gratuities For the Graduate

- *Write down your goals and dreams as a declaration to yourself. Let this be your own mission statement.*
- *Act enthusiastic and you will be enthusiastic.*
- *Limit your screen time viewing to a few hours per week.*
- *Avoid company gossip about your colleagues and the boss.*
- *Start each day ahead of schedule.*
- *Life isn't always fair, deal with it.*
- *Send handwritten notes instead of texting or emailing whenever possible.*
- *Look someone directly in the eyes when talking.*
- *Brush and floss.*
- *Laugh often, laugh loudly.*
- *Love all things and all people in your life lavishly. Love your family, your friends, your work and yourself.*
- *Place your family at the top of your to-do list.*

Dear Graduate

Written by Judy Smith
Photography by Lou Guarracino

Published by Holland Publishing
130 Thornhill Ln, Newtown, PA 18940
www.hollandpublishinggroup.com

Text copyright © 2015 by Judy Smith
Photography copyright © 2015 Lou Guarracino
Front cover photography: Dreamstime, Shutterstock

ISBN: 978-0-9961415-1-2
Library of Congress Control Number: Pending

Jacket design: Peri Poloni-Gabriel, Knockout Design, www.knockoutbooks.com
Interior design: Grace Savage, Savage Design, www.savagedesignstudios.com

Printed in Malaysia